PRE-WAR DOORMAN

by
Margaret Ryan

IBEX
New York

Book Design by Louise Kindley
Cover Illustration by Emily Ryan Lerner

Copyright © 2015 Margaret Ryan

All rights reserved. No part of this publication may be reproduced or transmitted in any form or by any means, electronic or mechanical, including photocopy, recording, or any information storage and retrieval system, without permission in writing from Ibex New York, ibexnewyork@gmail.com.

Printed in the United States of America
ISBN-13: 9780692472217

TABLE OF CONTENTS

Honeymoon 1

In the Flower Shop 2

The Marseilles 4

Bernini: Bacchanal: Faun Teased by Children 6

Abundance 7

A Walk on the Upper West Side 9

Straus Park 10

At Alice Underground 11

Physical Therapy: The Ansonia 12

Natural History 13

I Am Too Old to Live in Brooklyn 16

On Monday I Went to Sloan Kettering 17

Pastoral 18

Bad Back 19

Eviction Notice 20

After Christmas 21

Prometheus at Rockefeller Center 22

Classic Pre-War Doorman 2 Bedroom Apartment, Steps to Riverside Park!

Classic Pre-War Doorman building. Prime WEST END AVE 100s location, steps to 1 train, cafes, grocery and restaurants, Riverside Park. Top renovated prewar classic, lots of closets, high ceilings. 6th Floor. Entry foyer, living room, separate windowed kitchen with new appliances, countertop, dishwasher & microwave. Formal dining room, large bedroom with good southern city views and great natural light. Picture & crown moldings, many other fine pre-war details. Laundry room in building. Pets okay, live-in super. Charming tree-lined block.

New York Times

ACKNOWLEDGEMENTS

"Bernini: Bacchanal: Faun Teased by Children" appeared in *Poetry* magazine.

"On Monday I went to Sloan Kettering" appeared in *Mudfish*, under the title, "On Monday I went to the Hospital."

"Abundance" appeared in *Rattapallax 7*.

"Prometheus at Rockefeller Center" appeared in *The Beloit Poetry Journal*.

For my mother,
Anna Cornelia Jansen Ryan
1910-1999
and for all those others
who have opened doors for me

HONEYMOON

We wake together in a double bed.
Sunlight through shutters stripes the parquet floor.
Saturday. We're young, and newly wed.
We drink our coffee, hurry to the stores.

Columbus Avenue. United Meat.
It's early. Harold's apron's still pristine.
Behind glass cases, stainless cleavers gleam.
We buy a little chicken, stewing beef.

At Pioneer we get a solid block
of codfish for a chowder, a new mop,
Chock Full O'Nuts, Joy liquid, Ivory soap,
a jar of honey and a quart of milk.

Last stop, King Cole, the produce shop,
where Nate and Murray, grumpy, pear-shaped men
attend the fruit and cluck like Yiddish hens:
two golden apples and a cantaloupe.

IN THE FLOWER SHOP

Branches forced into bloom.
Leafless, skeletal, thorned,
with gray-brown bark. The flower,
five small peach-pink petals,
the cheeks of a white-skinned
child out too long in the cold.
The buds baroque pearls.

In the flower shop, quince
is the first indication of spring.
Never cheap, five gaunt sticks
can cost $150 in January. Larry,
who moved back to Michigan,
says no one sells quince there—
it grows wild, no one brings it in.

I remember in Laurie Colwin's
Family Happiness, an apartment
on Park Avenue, the family
clustered around the fireplace,
drinking chilled vermouth, the house
filled with forsythia and quince
and the hostess thinking

there was nothing so nice
as the sight of spring branches
near a wood fire. She was thrilled
it was snowing. Snow, a wood fire,
and flowering quince. The combination
her idea of perfection.
I have access to quince

at wholesale but never bring
a branch of it home. My apartment
on the west side is too small—quince
needs space to accentuate
its emaciation—and besides
I own no fireplace,
no grand piano. I prefer

a glass of Scotch, a mossy pan
of paperwhites, their greenery
and perfume occupying less space
than a cat on a cushion in the sun.

THE MARSEILLES

When we moved to the neighborhood,
snow covered the smashed-in roof.
Pigeons roosted in servants' quarters.
At night, the homeless broke in, lit fires—
smoke drifted from pane-less windows
above wrought-iron balconies.

Mr. Kay, the Broadway Barber—
Carrara marble, platinum mirrors,
milk-glass bottles marked Lavender
Water, Witch Hazel—said the Marseilles
was grand, like the Waldorf, once.
His shop held ten dark green leather chairs.

He worked alone and still had time to talk.
Hair was longer then. Unisex blow-dries
and rising rents could have driven him out,
but Mr. Kay had his clientele, including,
eventually, my husband. It was hard to think
of "grand" in our neighborhood,

with all the hippie places holding on,
Ahmahl's Whole Wheat Pizza, Uncle
Wong's Harbin Inn and the *comidas
Chinas y criollas* on every block—mostly
Chinese who fled from Cuba after Castro.
Black transvestites worked Broadway

in the 90's and further uptown Columbia
boys and Barnard girls huddled and laughed,
smoking as they exited the old West End,

jazz streaming out from behind the steam tables…
It was before Tom's Restaurant had a bit part
on Seinfeld. It was before Seinfeld.

Now it's hot. I can hear the hollow sound
of metal pipes dropped and lifted, dropped
again. They are erecting scaffolding around
another building. Another set of required repairs.
Another crumbling façade to be patched up,
bricks torn out to be underlain with insulation…

And it's hard not to applaud the renovation,
the fresh tile in the subway station, the gleaming
lobby of the Marseilles, now a residence
for the elderly poor, where we go twice
a year to vote. Ahmahl's is a Starbuck's.
Mr. Kay retired, donating his shop, entire,

to the Museum of the City of New York.
He died at 80, watching television
at home on the Upper East Side.

BERNINI: Bacchanal: Faun Teased by Children

A naked marble faun besieged by twins.
    Cheek to stone cheek, shoulder, elbow,
        apples, plums, the faun's hand
    grasping the rigid branch. A third child
trying to mount a hound's lean back.

I pace the pavane Bernini planned.
    I become the marble in his hand.
        And I have seen these marble boys before,
    cherubs napping in far galleries.
Slack-bellied, bronze, grouped around a tomb.

They wear the same mischief on their lips,
    Hinting at their power to undo. The dog
        stretches up as the grapes trail down.
    A lion's pelt is flung across the trunk.
The boys and faun carouse eternally. My daughter

lengthens into girl and rounds toward wife.
    I lose my little beauty by the hour.
        I'm past the telling moment of my life.
    The marble faun ascends the marble tree.
A lizard suns where everlastings bloom.

ABUNDANCE
Grand Army Plaza, Manhattan

The paving stones are laid in waves,
concentric, partial, spreading rings
in tones of black and gray and beige,
extended fans that overlap
like feathers on a pigeon's wing.

Like feathers on a pigeon's wing
the fountain's scalloped pools recede.
The broad dry shallow steps arise
by inches toward a naked green
bronze woman, stooped, with one bent knee.

She tries to rise from her bent knee.
At her left hip she lifts a tray.
Is it to show, or give away
her ample harvest — apples, plums?
Abundance leans toward Victory.

Across the square gilt Victory
strides forward on a granite base.
Winged and robed, she wears a crown
of olive branches interlaced.
Both her golden arms are raised.

With both her golden arms upraised,
she might be prow or figurehead
for lifelike Sherman on a horse
whose right rear hoof drives down to crush
a golden pine branch, needles spread.

A golden pine branch, needles shed
like feathers from a pigeon's wing.
The paving stones are laid in waves.
Naked, stooped, with bended knee,
Abundance yields to Victory.

A WALK ON THE UPPER WEST SIDE
or The Ornamentation of Architecture

So many details above doorways!
A frieze of acanthus leaves.
Façades festooned with fruit and sheaves
of wheat. Cupids at one cornice,
cartouches on the next, or lion's heads.
Limestone scallop shells in low relief.
Is this where the nature gods have flown:
apotheosis into stone?

Your amorous manner's like
a porte-cochère—elaborate,
outdated, draped with fruit
unfit for mortals. Don't press
your suit with me. I have observed:
what happens beyond rococo is absurd.

STRAUS PARK

April. Ginkgo fans
bright green
against dark bark.

A man on a bench sleeps
below the bronze
monument, Memory

recumbent. Memory
looks down. The shallow
pool fills and overflows.

A barefoot child
splashes, another
writes with chalk

on paving stones.
A raggedy man
leaves a sleeve

of lilacs. Another
lights a single
votive, shields

the flame, sets it
down on stone. I leave
no stone, no flowers,

no candle burning.
I remember
washing your hair.

Your name brings tears.

AT ALICE UNDERGROUND

At the vintage clothing store my daughter
walks among the mothballed black wool coats
with good mink collars. A child of spring,
she is unearthing piece by piece
my college wardrobe—T-shirts, bulky sweaters,
boot-cut jeans. She takes worn denim
between thumb and finger. I recognize
a kind of ravishment.

Fifteen, I loved my mother's Thirties,
searched second-hands for peplums, T-straps,
bias-cut skirts in pomegranate wool.
Now my daughter picks bright acrylic blouses
from a bin marked "Sixties—Special."
The grim man who takes both cash and credit
quiets the dog, a one-eyed Malamute.

Back home, my daughter brings tea,
confesses that she wants to dye
my red silk black, close the back
with little stitches. In her kingdom,
I have fallen from queen to faded
seamstress, as my mother, breathless
in a cotton wrapper, slides toward the rim of time.

Once I carried my light into her closet:
taffeta rustled like green leaves. Now
my mother's clothes are husks,
my daughter in her mother's habit.

PHYSICAL THERAPY: THE ANSONIA

Pomegranates among the capitals.
Ubiquitous bellflowers under the portico.
Frigid May. Just as well the flowers are chiseled
out of granite. Cyclamen planted at the foot
of the porch—some resident's idea of spring
brightening—lie frozen. Last week's late snow.
A skeleton pattern on the leaves. My skeleton
—new inflexibilities, disquiets, when I wake.
Another birthday. More paper-work. This week
my husband's 65. Medicare, half-price subway fares.
I can't say old age, not yet. But older is, so far,
a piebald plot. We are glad our pitfall bodies
have brought us here. But wish
fruits and flowers had not turned to stone.

NATURAL HISTORY

1.
I pace past skeletons
of dinosaurs, around
an enormous hall
remembering you

were always late. Light
pours in through small
high windows, thick,
honey-colored,

and I think of insects
trapped and preserved
in amber, immortality
I did not want.

Waiting I was trapped
in time, a time I believed
in love, or its likeness.

Specimen: a woman
wanting to be seen,
and listened to.

2.
I remember waiting
at bus stops, on subway
platforms, in restaurants.
I see myself holding

a table against the imperious

stares of a pair of waiters
in a hot spot downtown.
The waiters watch me sip

Chablis, watch their tips
evaporate, even as I imagine
you materializing, laughing
like Pan or Bacchus, trailing

your air of madder music,
stronger wine...

3.
In those days, I made a study of love.
Irritation, enervation, toxemia...
the progress of disease, but what's
the difference? Unable to eat or sleep,
I listened to opera with a fresh
sense of consequence: attending
a performance of *Lucia* at the miniature
Amato, I realized most love ends
unhappily, and though I would not
go mad, I would not be spared.

4.
You come, finally, lumbering,
an old bear just out of hibernation,
entering the hall of dinosaurs, dropping
apologies for being late.

We are not here to study skeletons
or stare into dioramas of vanished peoples
or even to covet the Star of India, the largest

sapphire in the world. We have met to learn

about space time, gravity the central fact.
Dented by heavenly bodies, space bends
pulling everything around it down, as bodies
on a mattress slide toward one another

as your lips fell toward mine.... Letters
to and from Einstein. In one he sketched
a man upside down as the earth turned,
a stick figure like a child would draw.

In another he wrote that falling in love
is not the most stupid thing people do,
but gravitation cannot be held responsible for it.

5.
Who was accountable for what happened
between us? An array of scenes played
to white tablecloths, to bar tables carved
with the names of previous lovers?

We leave the Great Hall. The light
is deeper and we kiss goodbye
the way stars explode, without
passion, without regret.

I AM TOO OLD TO LIVE IN BROOKLYN

to shop at Anthropologie,
to make artisanal pickles
and sell them at flea markets and
craft fairs. To eat most of my meals
from food trucks. To wear big skirts
and chandelier earrings and tattoos.
Still I got to wear bellbottoms
when they made their first appearance
since World War II – I had my dad's
original Navy pants, blue
Melton with 13 buttons on
the broadfall, his regulation
pea coat. And there were sit-ins on
College Hall Green and new Beatles
albums, Bob Dylan and marches
against the War on Washington
and the boycott of classes when
Nixon invaded Cambodia.
I was tear gassed at the Lincoln
Memorial. I can't really complain.

ON MONDAY I WENT TO SLOAN KETTERING
for Treat Davidson

You stood near the window, swollen, sagging.
The voice that announced,
"My mouth is filled with sores," was not yours.
Nor was I myself: gloved, gowned, masked.

You turned to your afternoon's task:
swallowing these pills with the nectar,
those with the bright red Jell-O.
I remembered the day we picked raspberries.

You were too sick to come. Your husband
and mine and our daughters worked in sun
under high clouds, a light wind lifting
leaves in the nearby woods.

The berries were creamy pink, clear scarlet,
blood red and nearly black. It was life
without you: your girls and mine running
through long rows, hurling berries, laughing,

stuffing their mouths with fruit.
I returned to the present. You were vomiting
something green into a stainless steel pan.
I rang for the nurse.

You said, "I'm sorry." I begged,
what can I do? "You've done it," you said,
leaning against pillows, your eyes closed.
"When it's your turn, I'll visit you."

PASTORAL

A block away a jackhammer hits the street.
Inside, aroused by heat, the radiator clangs.
On the phone, my daughter says Tylenol's
the cure for existential dread—that, or the live
puppy-cam she's found: explore.org.
I think of my grandfather's drop-front desk,
its mahogany honeycomb of drawers, a cache
of colored pencils, pen nibs, blotting paper,
a hidden compartment concealing only
LePage's mucilage, a medium for color.
And of the aromatics I'll toss into tonight's
stew, fresh thyme, parsley preserved in ice.
Seven years, and the scar over my husband's
heart is almost healed. My favorite pattern?
Toile, that repetitive depiction of the pastoral.
Blue-blooded shepherds and their high-haired
ladies engraved on copper, printed on fine-milled linen.

BAD BACK

Study the ceiling's aging plaster.
Experience the pain for information –
what makes it better or worse?
Drifting on a mild narcotic tide, notice
how light crafts shadows on the wall,
making of concrete objects disembodied stains.
Think of Pascal: *The present usually hurts.*
Imagine Tiepolo clouds on the ceiling,
lunch in a Paris tearoom, or, if you must,
recall a small girl on the downtown bus,
kicking and whining. And the woman
finally turning from her iPhone, asking
You want me to slap you? Pink dress, pigtails,
sparkles on sneakers—watch the girl sink
into herself, still as the eye of a storm.
Eyes closed, motionless, that girl goes
where no rhetoric can reach. Shimmers
as she ages into rage. Animal gathering
strength to strike, breathe into the pain
you have become. Focus, the masters tell us,
and it might disappear. Picture the teens
loitering on your corner, selling loosies,
forties, joints. Drugged to spare, who are you
to wish for children strong enough to stand?
Breathe and wait. Soon the throb you are
will be a memory, a museum you won't revisit,
the back of a slow bus disappearing down Broadway.

EVICTION NOTICE

We saw the moving men taking his things
just before Christmas, and they were nervous
when we came to the door—*Do you live here?*

Is this your place? They didn't want to be
confronted, didn't want to have to defend
what they were doing, *only making a living,*

Jack. And we who had lived six floors above
for more than thirty years, and said hello
and good evening and we're sorry

when his mother died, and helped him move
her piano onto the sidewalk, where for days
strangers played a peculiar medley of tunes—

we barely knew his name, had no way
to contact him and say, what happened,
we're sorry, can we help? So this morning

as snow fell, when I saw him round the corner,
it was as if the dead had risen, and we
embraced like long-lost brother and sister,

and he laughed and said, Those bastards,
and I said, Rodley, welcome home.

AFTER CHRISTMAS

Stripped of ornaments, we carry
the Christmas tree down to the lobby
and out to the curb then head back up
the elevator to pack the decorations,
the funny wooden toys we bought
when the baby, now 35, was a year old,
and the tin stars from a folk art fair,
and the reindeer fashioned from homemade
PlayDoh. The lights are tightly wound
around plastic spools designed
to keep swearing to a minimum next year
when the boxes come out again,
and we marvel again at the homemade
stockings and the glass baubles that survive.
Gifts, unboxed, have worked their way
into our wardrobes, and the days grow
if only by moments. And January
welcomes us back to monotony, winding
its gray wool scarf around our throats.

PROMETHEUS AT ROCKEFELLER CENTER

Power comes from the knees, my teacher says,
and I believe it. Power, power, power
my blades sing as they send me speeding.

Behind glass, at the edge of ice, eye level,
businessmen at lunch wave and smile.
I watch them sip their wine as I flash past.

Pale crumbs tumble from baguette to table.
One touch can change the known world into ash—
cherry in the woodstove proves it.

Be still, flames whisper. Wait and it will pass.
I will survive desire, or will lose it.
My body thinks, curves backward on a blade.

My arms embrace the circle that I've made.
Balanced on a blade of tempered steel,
I spin in place. Gravity is not my enemy.

The truth is I have stolen what's not mine.
Fire's used to soften metal.
I practice, becoming supple.

Grace is not freely given. Grace is won.
Or taken, then bestowed on those who need it.
The bells of St. Patrick's ring. My heart

is wrung. Their metal tongues are telling—
don't believe it. Up on Fifth Avenue, wearing

a sandwich board, bearing Corinthian epistles,

the man screams out again. *Fornicators
will burn. I destroy the wisdom of the wise.
Repent. Repent.* Ice is the sanity in me.

Back in the rink's center, I stretch my arms
toward Prometheus, the golden image.
Bend my knees and rise and turn again

to face facts as others face the altar.
Let men make their large gestures.
I am not powerless, or innocent.

Am not compelled to place a losing bet.
And short of a park view room,
the brut iced, the Beluga bursting,

this is as close to bliss as I can get.

www.ingramcontent.com/pod-product-compliance
Lightning Source LLC
Chambersburg PA
CBHW021002090426
42736CB00010B/1427